THE
ENGLISH LAKES
Wordsworth's Country

Painted by A. Heaton Cooper

THE SILVER STRAND, ULLSWATER

SALMON

Published by
J Salmon Limited
100 London Road, Sevenoaks,
Kent TN13 1BB

First edition 1994
Revised edition 1995
Designed by the Salmon Studio

Printed in England by
J Salmon Limited, Tubs Hill Works
Sevenoaks, Kent

DUNGEON GHYLL FORCE, GREAT LANGDALE

Coloured Illustrations

With exultation at my feet I saw
Lake, islands, promontories, gleaming bays,
A universe of Nature's fairest forms
Proudly revealed.

William Wordsworth

WINDERMERE

Unsurpassed for beauty and variety of scenery, Lake Windermere is the largest expanse of still water in England, stretching for ten miles from Lakeside in the south to Waterhead in the north. The lake is studded with small islands and surrounded by thickly wooded countryside. Important as habitat for lakeland wildlife, the woodland also provides shady walks and an effective backdrop to the waters of Windermere. From nearby Lowwood there are magnificent views towards Loughrigg Fell and the Langdale Pikes which tower above the waters of the lake to the northwest. The town of Windermere expanded and prospered after the coming of the railway in the mid-19th century. Today it is a popular centre for visitors while the lake itself provides a superb stretch of water for sailing and boating.

WINDERMERE FROM WANSFELL
Sunset

WINDERMERE AND THE LANGDALE PIKES FROM LOWWOOD
Sunshine after rain

THE SWAN INN, NEWBY BRIDGE

And there I sit at evening, when the steep
Of Silver Howe, and Grasmere's peaceful lake
And one green island, gleam beneath the stems
Of dark firs, a visionary scene.

William Wordsworth

GRASMERE

Set in a valley surrounded by hills, Grasmere was described by
Wordsworth as "the loveliest spot that man hath ever found".
The village itself lies north of the lake which is hemmed in on
all sides by fells which slope up from the wooded shores. The
medieval Parish Church of St. Oswald is a rough-cast building
with a heavily timbered roof. In the churchyard William
Wordsworth and several of his family, including his wife and
Dora, his daughter, lie buried. Close to the village is Dove
Cottage, the home of Wordsworth for nine years from 1799.
Here, during the period called his "Golden Decade", he wrote
many of his finest poems and today the cottage, little altered, is
preserved as a museum to his life and work.

A GLIMPSE OF GRASMERE

DOVE COTTAGE, GRASMERE

GRASMERE CHURCH

Sweet are the sounds that mingle from afar,
Heard by calm lakes, as peeps the folding star.
William Wordsworth

RYDAL WATER

Now protected by the National Trust, Rydal Water is one of the smallest yet most attractive of the lakes. Being largely obscured from the main road by trees, its beauties are often overlooked by the passing visitor and it is best approached either from Loughrigg or from White Moss Common. The River Rothay links Rydal Water to Windermere a few miles to the south. William Wordsworth lived at Rydal Mount from 1813 until his death in 1850 and the house, which is still owned by his descendants, contains interesting memorabilia of the poet. Next to the house, with its delightful gardens, is Dora's Field. This was given by Wordsworth to his daughter Dora and is famous for its springtime carpet of daffodils.

SUNSET, RYDAL WATER

Full many a spot
Of hidden beauty have I chanced to espy
Among the mountains; never one like this
So lonesome, and so perfectly secure.

William Wordsworth

THE LANGDALES

A tour of the Great and Little Langdale Valleys provides one of
the scenic wonders of the Lake District. As the head of the
valley is approached, the mountains close in on either side. To
the right are the distinctive twin peaks of the Langdale Pikes:
Harrison Stickle and Pike o' Stickle. Elterwater is one of the
smallest lakes and nearby is Skelwith Force where the
combined waters of the Langdale Beck and the River Brathay
rush headlong between rocky banks over a 15 feet drop. It is
particularly impressive after heavy rain. Blea Tarn nestles on
top of the ridge above the Little Langdale Valley. Beloved by
artists and photographers, it presents a perfect setting, with fir
trees and rhododendrons at the lakeside and the Langdale Pikes
mirrored in its placid waters.

ELTERWATER AND THE LANGDALE PIKES

SKELWITH FORCE, RIVER BRATHAY

BLEA TARN AND THE LANGDALE PIKES

. . . lustily
I dipped my oars into the silent lake,
And, as I rose upon the stroke, my boat
Went heaving through the water like a swan.
William Wordsworth

CONISTON AND HAWKSHEAD

Coniston Water lies parallel to Windermere and is one of the most beautiful of the lakes, with wooded fells coming down to the water's edge. Pretty little Fir Island and Peel Island nestle under the eastern shore. Dominating the five mile long lake is the striking peak known as the Old Man of Coniston. Its flanks are somewhat scarred with disused quarries and mines but the views from the summit are excellent. Coniston village is situated at the northern end of the lake and is a good centre for excursions. In the vale of Esthwaite, between Coniston and Windermere lies Esthwaite Water with the picturesque village of Hawkshead nearby. With its narrow streets, quaint white-washed cottages, stone steps, squares and courtyards, Hawkshead is one of the most delightful places in the district.

CHARCOAL BURNERS, CONISTON WATER

BRANTWOOD, CONISTON WATER
Char fishing at sunset

THE OLD BUTCHER'S SHOP, CONISTON

AN OLD STREET IN HAWKSHEAD

APPLE BLOSSOM, ESTHWAITE WATER

In depth, in height, in circuit, how serene
The spectacle, how pure!–Of Nature's works,
In earth, and air, and earth-embracing sea,
A revelation infinite it seems.

William Wordsworth

WASTWATER

The parish of Wasdale Head, with its picturesque beck and packhorse bridge, is said to contain England's highest mountain, deepest lake and smallest church. Remote Wastwater lies in the wildest situation of all the lakes and, being 258 feet deep, it is also the deepest. On its southern shore massive screes plunge sheer into the water but on the north side the shore is more approachable and there are magnificent views towards the head of the lake where it is dominated by the peaks of Great Gable and Scafell Pike. Beyond Eskdale and Harter Fell to the south-east, is the picturesque valley of the River Duddon. Near the hamlet of Seathwaite stepping stones traverse the rushing waters.

WASTWATER FROM THE STRANDS

STEPPING STONES, SEATHWAITE

WASDALE HEAD AND GREAT GABLE
Towards evening in autumn

There's joy in the mountains;
There's life in the fountains,
Small clouds are sailing,
Blue sky prevailing;
The rain is over and gone
William Wordsworth

BUTTERMERE AND CRUMMOCK WATER

At the western end of the Honister Pass are Buttermere and Crummock Water. These two lakes are separated by a narrow strip of meadow-land and cradled by a wild and romantic valley. Although it is one of the smaller lakes in the district, Buttermere is nonetheless one of the more spectacular. It is situated 250 feet above sea level and is ringed on three sides by mountains, including the dramatic peaks of Melbreak, Haystacks and Fleetwith Pike. Crummock Water, below Buttermere, is a delightful stretch of water in impressively rugged surroundings. Mountains rise from the water's edge and the valley is protected by the National Trust. Lying on the north-west edge of the Lake District, Loweswater is closely enfolded in mountains and situated in a prettily wooded valley.

THE HEAD OF BUTTERMERE

THE OLD POST OFFICE, LOWESWATER

CRUMMOCK WATER FROM SCALE HILL

All things that love the sun are out of doors;
The sky rejoices in the morning's birth;
The grass is bright with rain-drops.

William Wordsworth

DERWENTWATER AND BORROWDALE

Considered to be one of the loveliest of all the lakes, Derwentwater is surrounded by green fells, steep crags and feathery woods. The surface of the lake is dotted with little wooded islands which seem to float on the glassy waters and picturesque beauty spots abound on the lake's shores. The stunningly beautiful valley of Borrowdale, its wooded slopes topped by towering crags, follows the course of the River Derwent before rising over rugged Honister Pass. The road, which leads to Buttermere, here reaches 1,176 feet above sea level. At the foot of the valley is the hamlet of Grange-in-Borrowdale with its pretty stone bridges over the Derwent. About a mile from Grange, above the south-east corner of Derwentwater, are the famous Lodore Falls where the stream tumbles down a tree-hung ravine.

LODORE AND DERWENTWATER
A summer's morn

DERWENTWATER FROM CASTLE HEAD
A bright morning

FALCON CRAG, DERWENTWATER

HONISTER PASS AND BUTTERMERE

GRANGE IN BORROWDALE
Early morning

There was a time when meadow, grove and stream,
The earth and every common sight,
To me did seem
Apparelled in celestial light.

William Wordsworth

KESWICK

Situated on the River Greta at the far northern extremity of Derwentwater, Keswick is an attractive old market town. Its narrow streets and sturdy grey stone buildings, including the notable Moot Hall of 1813, are sheltered beneath the 3,054 feet high slopes of Skiddaw. Keswick is the principal centre for visiting both Derwentwater and Borrowdale, which lie just to the south. The Parish Church of St. Kentigern at Crosthwaite is one of the most important centres of early Christian worship and is the only church in England which has a full set of twelve consecration crosses carved in the walls. Crosthwaite Church also contains some notable monuments including one to the poet Robert Southey who was a regular worshipper here and is buried in the churchyard.

CROSTHWAITE CHURCH, KESWICK

Oh, there is blessing in this gentle breeze
A vis'tant that while it fans my cheek
Doth seem half-conscious of the joy it brings
From the green fields, and from yon azure sky.

William Wordsworth

BASSENTHWAITE LAKE

Four miles long Bassenthwaite, the most northerly lake in the Lake District, is also the fourth largest area of water in the National Park. The road from Keswick to Carlisle follows the eastern shore of the lake under the shadow of mighty Skiddaw and passes Bassenthwaite village near the north-eastern corner. The parish church which still retains its Norman chancel arch is a 12th or 13th century foundation. It stands alone at the end of a track three miles south of the village in a field near the lake shore. In common with many of the lakes, Bassenthwaite is popular with yachtsmen and fishermen but the interests of nature conservation have first priority. The lake is often visited by migrating birds and the vendace, one of Britain's rarest fishes, is found only in Bassenthwaite and Derwentwater.

BASSENTHWAITE LAKE
A breezy morn

I wandered lonely as a cloud
That floats on high o'er vales and hills
When all at once I saw a crowd,
A host, of golden daffodils.

William Wordsworth

ULLSWATER

Second largest of the lakes, Ullswater is 7½ miles long and is composed of three reaches which zig-zag between impressive mountains. It lies to the north of Windermere beyond the rugged Kirkstone Pass, an impressive, rock-strewn cleft, 1,500 feet above sea level. Descending towards Patterdale and Ullswater, the road passes the little lake of Brothers Water. One of Ullswater's principal beauty spots is Gowbarrow Fell which lies on the northern side of the lake and affords wonderful views in all directions. It was a springtime visit to Gowbarrow Park which inspired Wordsworth's famous poem "The Daffodils". Surrounded by lovely lakeside woodlands and hill farms, Ullswater is a popular sailing centre and steamers ply the length of the lake from Glenridding Pier to Pooley Bridge.

KIRKSTONE PASS AND BROTHERS WATER

SILVER BAY, ULLSWATER

ULLSWATER FROM GOWBARROW PARK
A sultry June morn

There sometimes doth a leaping fish
Send through the tarn a lonely cheer;
The crags repeat the raven's croak.

William Wordsworth

THIRLMERE AND HAWESWATER

Mid-way between Ambleside and Keswick in the shadow of mighty Helvellyn, lies Thirlmere. The road from Windermere passes along the eastern shore of the lake, providing many delightful vistas across the water to where wooded Raven Crag rears up on the far side. This picturesque lake serves as a reservoir providing water for the city of Manchester. The supply is augmented by Haweswater, another reservoir created by enlarging a natural lake. The area has undergone dramatic changes in the last hundred years. Lakeside farms and fields have disappeared and new roads and footpaths have been created. An inn beside Thirlmere, where Wordsworth and Coleridge used to meet, is now submerged beneath the waters.

RAVEN CRAG, THIRLMERE

HAWESWATER